Labor Day

by Meredith Dash

capstone®

ABDO
NATIONAL HOLIDAYS
Kids

Photo Credits: Alamy, Getty Images, Old Oregon Photos, Shutterstock, Thinkstock, © Kelly Short, Lewis W. Hine / CC-BY-SA-2.0 p.7, © Iakov Filimonov / Shutterstock.com p.21

Production Contributors: Teddy Borth, Jennie Forsberg, Grace Hansen

Design Contributors: Candice Keimig, Laura Rask, Dorothy Toth

Library of Congress Cataloging-in-Publication data is available on the Library of Congress Website.

ISBN 978-1-4966-0993-9 (paperback)

Printed and bound in the USA.
009942F16

Table of Contents

Labor Day

Labor Day **honors** American workers. Workers make our nation strong.

5

History

People worked very

long days in the 1800s.

Even children worked.

It was a hard life.

6

7

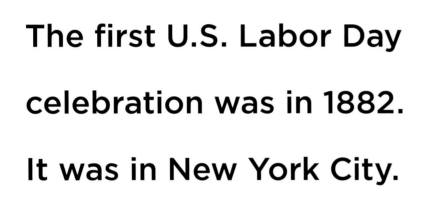

The first U.S. Labor Day

celebration was in 1882.

It was in New York City.

9

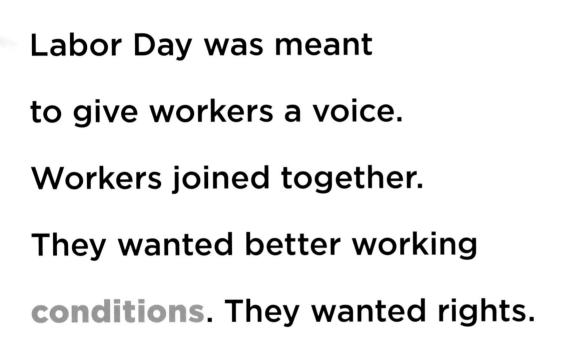

Labor Day was meant
to give workers a voice.
Workers joined together.
They wanted better working
conditions. They wanted rights.

10

11

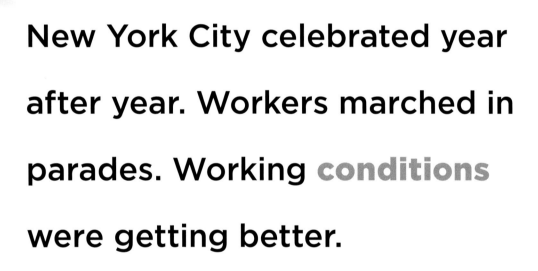

New York City celebrated year after year. Workers marched in parades. Working **conditions** were getting better.

13

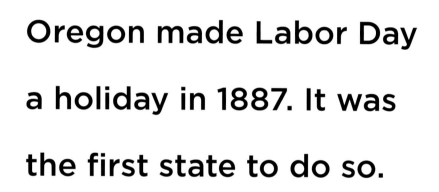

Oregon made Labor Day
a holiday in 1887. It was
the first state to do so.

15

On June 28, 1894, Labor Day

became a **national holiday**.

President Grover Cleveland

signed it into law.

16

17

Today's Labor Day

We celebrate Labor Day on the first Monday in September. Workers **enjoy** a day off from work.

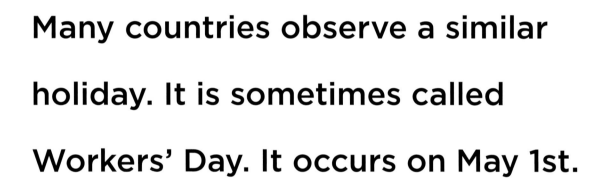

Many countries observe a similar holiday. It is sometimes called Workers' Day. It occurs on May 1st.

More Facts

- A long time ago, workers were paid very little and worked very long days. Even small children worked.

- Originally, Labor Day was used as a day to discuss plans for better working conditions.

- Today, Labor Day is a day for workers to relax and feel appreciated!

Glossary

condition – the way something is.

enjoy – to find happiness in.

honor – to pay respect to.

national holiday – a special event celebrated by a country.

Index